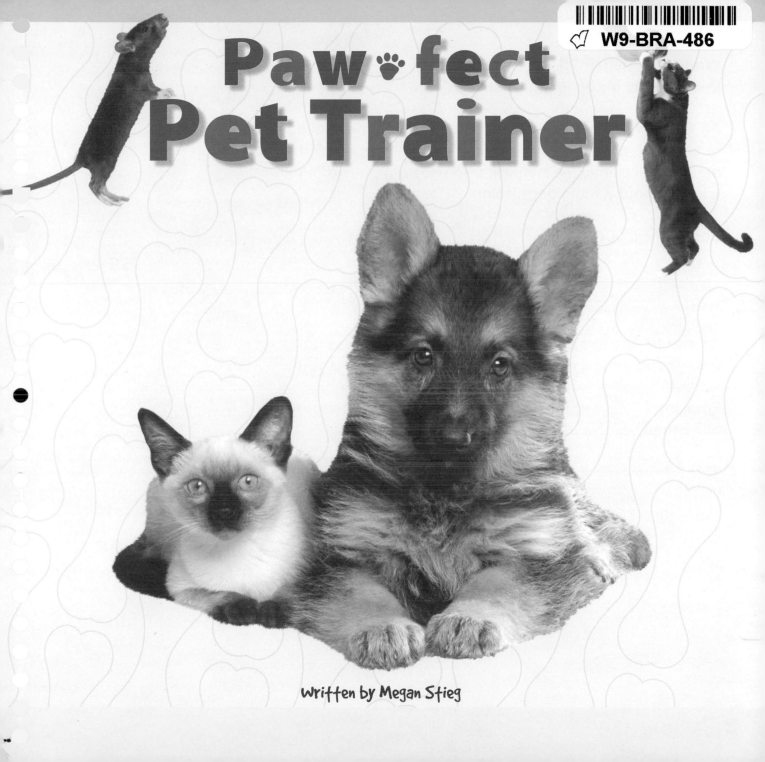

Paw●fect Pet Trainer

Written by Megan Stieg

Written by Megan Stieg
Designed by Michelle Martinez Design, Inc.

an imprint of
SCHOLASTIC
www.scholastic.com

Published by Tangerine Press, an imprint of Scholastic Inc., 557 Broadway; New York, NY 10012

10 9 8 7 6 5 4 3 2 1

ISBN-10: 0-545-14562-7
ISBN-13: 978-0-545-14562-6

Made in China

What's Inside

Introduction

Animals can do amazing stunts. Some dogs and cats know how to roll over on command or jump through hoops, and some hamsters can balance on their hind legs. How do you get your pet to do cool tricks like these? This book, along with the clicker included in your kit, shows you how to turn your pet into a stunt superstar!

How Animals Learn

When pets learn by experience, it's called *classical conditioning*. If something makes them happy, they want to do it again! But if something hurts or frightens them, animals will avoid it.

Pets also learn by observation—they watch what's going on around them. So, you may have to show your pet how the tricks are done. They'll learn by watching you!

In the early 1900s, a Russian scientist named Ivan Pavlov studied dogs and their behavior. He rang a bell when it was time to feed the dogs. After a while, every time the bell rang, the dogs would start drooling like crazy. They had learned that the bell meant food!

The Basics

It's time to make your pet a stunt star!
But first, there are a few things that you
need to know:

Use the clicker
Click it when your pet moves in the right direction or behaves the way you
want. Your pet will learn that the sound of the clicker means "good job!"

Be consistent
Use the same command to help
your pet remember the trick, just like
Pavlov's dog!

trainer tip

Start your commands by saying
your pet's name. That way, you'll
have your pet's attention!

Keep it simple
Short, clear commands help your pet stay focused.

Pour on the praise
After a training session, give your pet some of its favorite treats,
pat its fur, and show your pet how pleased you are.

Keep it short
Pets have a short attention span, so spend no more than 15 minutes at
a time practicing with them.

Basic Commands
Before you teach your dog the tricks in this book, make sure that your
dog has mastered some basic commands like Sit, Stay, and Down.

What Not to Do

★ Don't yell if your pet doesn't get it right! Getting mad only makes training go slower.

★ Don't train in places that are loud and full of distractions.

★ Don't have a training session right after your pet eats. Your pet will get an upset stomach.

★ Don't try teaching your pet new tricks until it feels comfortable with you.

Easy Tricks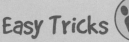

It shouldn't take your pet too long to get these tricks.

Medium Tricks

Some pets may find these tricks a little more difficult, so be consistent and have patience.

Tricky Trick

It may take a while for your pet to learn these tricks.

trainer tip

Dogs and cats can both learn all of the tricks in this book. However, hamsters, gerbils, guinea pigs, and other rodents might have trouble with dog and cat tricks.

Dog Tricks

Dogs love learning tricks because they're smart. They also try hard to make their owners happy. You'll have tons of fun practicing these tricks together!

Hide Your Eyes

With this trick, you can get your dog to play peek-a-boo . . . or learn how to look away in embarrassment!

The trick

Get your dog to put a paw over its eyes whenever you give the command, "**Hide your eyes.**"

Pet Star Steps

1. Have your dog sit or lie down facing you.

2. Hold your clicker in one hand. Then, cover your eyes with your other hand while saying, "Hide your eyes."

3. After you've demonstrated the trick a few times, get your dog to try it: Gently pick up your pet's front leg and say, "Hide your eyes."

4. Press the clicker when you've lifted the paw up to your dog's eyes.

5. Then, praise your furry pal for a job well done!

Shake

How cool would it be to have your canine pal shake hands—er, paws—with you?

The trick

Your furry friend gives you a paw when you say, "**Shake**."

Pet Star Steps

1. Start out with your dog sitting.

2. Kneel down on the floor in front of your dog.

3. Hold the clicker in one hand and hold out your other hand like you're going to shake hands with someone. Give the command, "Shake."

4. Gently lift up your pup's front paw. Press the clicker.

5. Put your dog's paw back on the ground and give your furry friend a big hug!

Bang

This trick teaches your dog how to lie down and play dead.

The trick

When you point at your dog and say, **"Bang,"** your furry friend will fall to the ground and lie still.

Pet Star Steps

1. Start out with your dog sitting.

2. Stand in front of your pet and hold the clicker in one hand.

3. With the other hand, point at your dog. Give the command, "Bang!"

4. Gently help your dog to lie down on the floor and stay still.

5. When the dog is calmly lying down, press the clicker.

6. Give your puppy pal a lot of praise and a little treat.

trainer's tip

Usually, lightly pushing down a dog's rump will get him to sit. A little soft pressure on the shoulders after that should get him to lie down.

Light Off 🐾

Train your dog to be an energy saver! Get your fluffy pal to hit the lights!

The trick

Say, "Light off," and your furry friend will stand on its hind legs to turn off a light switch.

Attention

This trick is great for big dogs, but it's not recommended for small dogs.

Pet Star Steps

1. Make sure your dog is tall enough to reach the light switch.

2. Have your dog buddy sit by a light switch that is turned on.

3. Balance one of your buddy's favorite treats on top of the switch.

4. Give the command, "Light off."

5. When your dog stands up to get the treat, carefully help its paw to pull the switch down!

6. Press the clicker when your dog touches the switch.

trainer tip

It's better to reward your pet with a lot of praise and attention than treats. Too many treats could give your favorite furry friend a weight problem.

Cat Tricks

Cats have a mind of their own. But if you have a little patience, you CAN convince a stubborn cat to come around to doing tricks!

Come 🐾

This is a great trick for getting your cat to come to you.

The trick

Call your fluffy friend's name and give the command, "**Come**," and your pet will head right to you.

Pet Star Steps

1. Start by standing close to your cat.

2. Have the clicker in one hand and a treat in the other.

3. Call your cat's name and give the command, "Come."

4. Hold the treat out to your cat.

5. When your cat walks to you, press the clicker and give the treat.

6. Each time you practice, try calling your cat from a little farther away.

trainer tip

Cats respond well to praise and attention! If you are using treats for this trick, only practice it once or twice a day.

Up 🐾

With this trick, your kitty will do a little dance for you and your friends!

The trick

Say, "Up" and your kitty stands up on hind legs.

Pet Star Steps

1. Get your cat to sit in front of you.

2. Hold the clicker in one hand. Raise your other hand, palm down, fingers together, and give the command, "Up."

3. Your cat will be curious about what is in your hand, so kitty will stand up to reach it.

4. When kitty stands, press the clicker.

5. Give a lot of praise and attention to kitty.

Roll Over

Your furry friend will show off by rolling over for you!

The trick

When you say, "Rollover," your kitty will roll from one side to the other.

This trick works for dogs, too!

Pet Star Steps

1. Start by getting your cat to lie down on its side.

2. Hold the clicker in one hand. Hold the other hand palm up.

3. Give the command, "Roll over" as you turn your palm down.

4. For the first couple of times, you may need to gently use your hands to roll your cat over.

5. When your kitty rolls over, press the clicker.

6. Give your furry friend praise for a job well done!

Jump

With this trick, your cat will become a jumping champion.

The trick

Hold a large hula hoop and say, "Jump." Your kitty will amaze your friends by jumping through the hoop.

Pet Star Steps

1. Ask a helper to hold a hula hoop so it touches the ground. Have your kitty sit on one side of the hoop.

2. While placing a treat on the ground on the other side of the hoop, give the command, "Jump."

3. Your cat should walk through the hoop to get to the treat. When kitty walks through the hoop, press the clicker.

4. Next time, have your helper hold the hoop a couple of inches off the ground. (Your cat should still be able to step over it.) Repeat step 2. Don't forget to press the clicker when kitty steps through the hoop!

5. Keep raising the hoop until your cat leaps right through when you say "Jump."

6. As soon as your furry friend can jump through the hoop without a treat, you can hold the hoop yourself.

Rodent Tricks

Before You Begin

Don't try any of these tricks until your pet rodent is used to being handled. Put your hand in the animal's cage and let your little buddy crawl onto your palm. Don't pick up your pet from above, and *never* pick it up by the tail!

Your furry little friends may not have big brains, but they have the smarts to learn a few nifty tricks! Whether your pet is a mouse, rat, hamster, gerbil, or Guinea pig, you can teach your little furry companion to become a miniature acrobat.

Attention

When you try to pick up a rodent from above, your hand looks like a giant predator to the rodent... really scary! Rodents will bite in defense, so be careful!

Up

Teach your furry friend to stand on its hind legs!

The trick

If you hold a little treat in one hand and give the "Up" command, your little buddy will stand on hind legs to get the treat.

Pet Star Steps

1. Hold the clicker in one hand and your pet's favorite snack in the other.

2. Hold the treat above your furry friend's head. Give the command, "Up."

3. Your pet will stand up to reach the treat.

4. When your little buddy is standing on hind legs, press the clicker, and give it the treat.

trainer tip

Rodents love sunflower seeds, nuts, vegetables, and fruit (but no citrus!). Find the snack your pet loves most.

Climb

Just think, your little rodent pal can sit on your shoulder to watch TV!

The trick

You say, "**Climb**," and your pet walks up your arm and sits on your shoulder.

A friend may need to help you set down the treats the first couple of times you try the trick.

Pet Star Steps

1. Hold the clicker in one hand. Gently hold your pet in the other hand.

2. Have your helper set a treat on your arm somewhere between the wrist and the elbow.

3. Put another one between your elbow and your shoulder, and put a third treat on your shoulder.

4. Give the command, "Climb," and let your pet walk up your arm to get the treats.

5. Press the clicker when your cuddly critter makes it to your shoulder.

Attention

Be sure to practice this trick while sitting on the floor, so if your pet falls off, it won't be such a bad landing!

Paw

Imagine how cool it would be to get your little pet to put its paw up to give you a high five!

The trick

With this trick, say, "**Paw**," and your pet holds out its front paw.

Pet Star Steps

1. Get your pet to stand up by using the "Up" command (see Page 19).

2. When your pet stands, hold out a treat a little higher than its head.

3. When your petite pal reaches out a paw to get it, press the clicker, and give the treat.

Your hairy little buddy may not want to hold still long enough to stand up and hold out its paw. Stick with it! The treats will help!

Competing in the Paws Olympics

trainer tip

Keep the entire competition under 15 minutes! You don't have to do all the events at once.

Show off all the cool things your pet has learned with these timed activities.

Sit-and-Stay Warm Up

Event One

trainer tip

You'll need a stop-watch or timer for this event.

What you do: Help your pet start the Paws Olympics with a concentration exercise. Tell your pet, **"Sit, Stay."** When it does, press the clicker and start the timer. Stop the timer when she lies down or gets up.

0-10 seconds
11-20 seconds
21 seconds or longer

Perfect Paws

0-2 shakes
3-4 shakes
5 or more shakes

Event Two

What you do: Give the **"Shake"** command. Count how many times in a row your pet will hold out its paw for you to shake. Don't forget to press the clicker each time your pet does it!

Hoop Hopping

0–6 inches (18 CM)

7–12 inches (18–30 CM)

More than 12 inches (30 CM)

Event Three

What you do: Hold the hoop on the ground. Give the **"Jump"** command. Raise the hoop every time you try the trick, and measure how high your pet will jump!

trainer tip

For this event, have a hoop big enough for your pet to jump through. Use a ruler to measure the height of the hoop.

Outrageous Obstacle Course

Event Four

What you do: Ask an adult to help you create a small obstacle course. Set up a sturdy box for your pet to climb over. Next, ask a friend to hold up a hoop for your pet to jump through. Finally, secure a cardboard box that's open on both ends so your pet can walk through it. Carefully lead your pet through the obstacle course while timing how long it takes with a stopwatch.

trainer tip

If your pet skips an obstacle, go back to the beginning of the course and start again.

More than 3 minutes

1–3 minutes

Less than 1 minute

Taking the Prize

Congratulations! You and your pet have put in a lot of hard work, so now it's time for a reward. Here's a ribbon to award your pet for an awesome performance! Then, fill out your trainer's certificate.

#1 Pet Star

Certificate

This certifies that

_____
(your name)

did an amazing
job training

_____
(pet name)

a _____
(pet type)

Congratulations! You are
now a star trainer!